STONE DRESS

for Rhona and Roger

August 2015

for Molly

Shirley McClure

with love from
Shirley x

STONE DRESS

ARLEN
HOUSE

Stone Dress

is published in 2015 by
ARLEN HOUSE
42 Grange Abbey Road
Baldoyle
Dublin 13
Ireland
Phone/Fax: 353 86 8207617
Email: arlenhouse@gmail.com
arlenhouse.blogspot.com

Distributed internationally by
SYRACUSE UNIVERSITY PRESS
621 Skytop Road, Suite 110
Syracuse, NY 13244–5290
Phone: 315–443–5534/Fax: 315–443–5545
Email: supress@syr.edu

978–1–85132–137–7, paperback

Typesetting by Arlen House

front cover image 'Solstice' by Rowan Gillespie
is reproduced courtesy of the artist
www.rowangillespie.com

back cover image by Caroline Schofield
is reproduced courtesy of the artist
www.carolineschofield.blogspot.ie

CONTENTS

STONE DRESS

BUDGET NIGHT

There is nothing on TV
except cost extraction strategies,
crisis cuts and cleverality.
You and I watch budget round-ups
from the old brown couch, endure
the sounds of less and less

until like semi-state bodies
we begin to merge, your right
meets my left despite the issues
of the day, alters its position
just a fraction, introduces
tried and tested measures.

The voices from the House
grow indistinct,
the old brown couch
becomes our Chamber,
there is no stopping
this amalgamation

as preferential interests are unveiled,
this fresh alliance
plunges past our thresholds,
shakes our standard rates,
leaves core weekly entitlements
untouched.

A MARRIAGE
after Anne Stevenson

When he gave us the biopsy results,
taut phrases gleaned from the handbook
of *How Not to Shock*,
you pretended illiteracy, made him retell
in layman's language, insisted on pictures.

Later, intact in the dark together,
I whispered, *I don't think we should marry now,*
but you repeated, *I wish we'd done it sooner,*
I wish I'd asked you sooner,
no way can you get out of this.

It was what's called an unreal time,
yet more immediate, more lived in
than the café days that followed.
You bought me blue pyjamas,
rewashed and berry-scented nightly.

At home we made delicate love,
watchful of bandages,
you allowed me to lament,
allowed me to imagine
a life with you.

ENGAGEMENT

Nurse dresses the wound,
we talk hormones, oestrogen,
how the levels will drop
like water in a summer pool
that yields only a dry ring,
a glaze of salt.

She says I can swim in salt
water, now that the wound
is healing; she says to ring
if there's a problem. Oestrogen
used to be my friend. The pool
is out of bounds, but I can drop

down into the waves, swim till I drop,
crawl out covered in salt.
Sea water gathers in a pool
at my feet, and even the wound
shines. Sunbathers beam oestrogen,
and I stand, hopeless in a ring

of bare-breasted women. Can't ring
any nurse about this. Can't drop
out of the world because of oestrogen.
I change in our room, taste salt.
My sun dress won't cover the wound,
I pull on an old t-shirt, curl up by the pool.

You find me at the pool.
Still not used to your ring –
the ring came before the wound,
before the floor dropped
out of the world, before salt
baths and the war against oestrogen.

Was it the oestrogen
you fell for, or the reflecting pool,
or my image conserved in salt?
Would you rather I gave back the ring,
would you rather we dropped
the whole plan? I wound

you with questions, wound with oestrogen,
the drops I have left, run from the pool,
your ring glued to my finger with salt.

THE ARGUMENT FOR CHEMOTHERAPY

Imagine we wanted
to knock down this wall,
says the doctor.
This pen is the hammer,
which represents the tablets.

And he begins to
tap tap tap
with his ball-point pen
on the cool white wall
beside his desk.

I wonder who's next door,
an intern with a headache
or another imagistic doctor,
rapping for *her* patients' benefit
on the opposite side,

till one day,
many demonstrations
down the road,
a keyhole of hope
is exposed.

Eventually,
he rests his silver biro
on my case notes, *we would*
break down the wall.
But what if, and he stands,

I took a sledgehammer?
He swipes with tailored jacket arms,
a Victorian High Striker, a Thor:
Now you see what happens
to the wall?

PHOTO SHOOT

Standing topless in the black box,
I pull my tummy in and hold my number up,
the hospital photographer makes pictures
of my newly-pinked right nipple.

Nurses rave about the handiwork,
scars are praised,
micro-pigmentation applauded,
yours is the best we've taken.

Never has my breast received so much attention,
maybe someday it will grace the pages
of *Plasthetics* magazine.
There is more than one way to find fame.

SPECIALISTS

Driving to St James's in a thunderstorm –
at the canal there's a new pink sign:

Hand and Foot Spa. Terms like callus peel,
gel overlay, make me wince.

At the Breast Clinic, a nurse I haven't seen
for a year examines me. *Ah yes*, she smiles,

I remember your scar: how it ends
in a V there under the axilla.

He was proud of that. I recall the surgeon
unveiling his signature finish

to a group of students. *Funny*, says the nurse,
what makes some people tick.

MISSING PARTS

That Easter holidays my father
had his thin, stained teeth forked out.
He had to learn to speak and eat again
before the summer term,

all with a plastic cart in his mouth.
I could not see ahead, I almost died
when one of the boys in my class asked:
'What's up with your dad? He's talking funny'.

Now me, in flimsy pink pyjamas –
heaviest thing I can bear –
unable to conceal the sudden flatness
of the right side of my chest.

A colleague visits me in hospital.
I have been coping without mirrors,
I'm not ready for him yet,
his eyes fast-tracking from my face

to the small roundness of a bandage
not making up for the fullness on my left.
His shocked male stare
like a schoolboy, reading me.

APTITUDE TEST

Turn left; no, right; no, left;
I prompt him as,
never great at telling
the difference,
I am doubly, no, trebly confused
by these wrong-sided cars,
these back-to-front highways,
these schematic maps.

In psychometric tests
I score poorly
on spatial awareness;
and the only thing worse,
at a party, than someone
outlining the stages of a recipe –
no pen or paper, no way
I'll remember –
are helpful directions like:
turn right after the cast-iron railings;
eighteenth bungalow on the same side
as the church. You'll see
my car outside,
you know, the Skoda ...

The funny thing is,
since the mastectomy,
despite numbness, lopsidedness
and scars, I sometimes forget
which side it was,
really forget inside my body,
not simply the words in my head
for right; no, left; no, right.

STONE DRESS

Her whole body was covered with a skin hard as rock.
She was sometimes called Stone-dress.
– The Spear-Finger, Cherokee myth

When she lay by the pool,
her children would hopscotch along her,

chalking her body from one to home,
giggle as they landed

on the pebbles of her kneecaps,
the limestone of her chest.

When she baked fruitcake,
standing in her apron by the oven,

her thighs and her belly would heat
to a hundred degrees;

so when the book club arrived,
they would peel off their scarves

and their cashmere cardigans,
their knee-high boots and their skirts.

By the time they had analysed the plot,
knocked back the wine and cake,

they were all sitting naked
in the peppery room.

This was where she felt safest,
in the landscape of their folds and scars;

no jokes about her hard neck, thick skin,
here in the stone circle of her friends.

LABELS

The woman ahead of me
in the queue for Customer Services
at the Bank of Ireland
has folded up her copper high-lit hair

so you can read
the Gothic characters sunk in
to the fair skin and fat that mask
her first thoracic vertebra:

splayed out between
the curve of neck and rim
of her black t-shirt – Robbie,
just where a label would be.

I think of Robbie, cushioned
by the bolster of her back, intact
in his indelibility, and wonder
has he, too, absorbed

this lover's name –
Shania, Sasha or Sinéad –
under the hood
of his Quiksilver hoodie?

Or has he a line
of Limited Edition lovers
scattered over Dublin, each one
bearing his brand?

GROOMED

Today she has been clipped, primped, squeezed,
handed back with a pink bow. She's a smooth black angel
beneath whose sleek chops, butter wouldn't melt.

Tonight is warm, the garden wild with possibility.
Suddenly the bellows of her belly surge, her body spasms
to expel the rare meat struggling in her mouth.

On the grass the hedgehog still breathes, but somehow
she has opened him, got right in without incurring
a single spine on her perfectly-barbered snout.

PROPOSAL

I don't suppose you'd marry me,
says the painter, as I draw circles
with his shoulder, trace a curving channel
from the shade of his axilla
to the rimple at his wrist.

Proposals in this job are rare.
There are the guys who whisper:
Squeeze my arches and I'll give you
anything you want; and the chancers:
groin strain; bother with me glutes.

But most men know this is worth
lying down for, staying still for.
My cook friend gets asked all the time,
guys fall in love with her Spicy Aioli;
she takes it with a pinch of salt.

When he is healed, the artist
presents me with a painting: Slea Head
in the background; the foreground, he admits,
is fantastical: a jungle-fringed path;
a young woman, hand on her Panama hat,

the other holding that of a child.
He tells me the woman is me,
the girl my niece – he's invented a niece –
both slim as Guinea grass, they gaze out
at an impossible ocean.

AFTER THE MASSAGE

On a good day
a country woman
kisses my fingers.
These hands, she hallows,
God bless these hands.

My plainsong palms
lie holy in her grasp;
choir girl thumbs
blink, blush, swell,
Is she talking about us?

THE DRIVING INSTRUCTOR

He was a man you wouldn't ordinarily
invite into your car.

Caress the gear stick, love,
imagine it's the boyfriend.

She wished she'd put her foot down
on the ABC of feminist first principles,

charged him to keep his chevrons
on his sleeve,

but stuck in his box junction,
she daren't let the lever leave her grasp.

She should have scorched the tyres
on the acutest hairpins of revenge

or done a *Thelma and Louise,*
ignoring contra-flows and *Danger – Cliffs.*

She should have leveled all his crossings,
made him yield at the first junction,

she should have told him: *Stop –*
this is my girlfriend's car.

ON READING TWO POETS

The prescribed text
presses forward its full chest
of complicated verses,
a proud half-smile

on its scarcely-opened lips,
confident that if I give it time,
read up on the Romans
– Wikipedia at least –

I too will be Pulitzered,
by the associative, sonic
and formal properties rustling
beyond mere denotation.

Instead I'm reading you,
page after naked page
swallowing your poems,
wiping their juices

from the edges of my mouth,
asking myself,
is there something wrong
if it's easy?

THE KISS

I could have been
a better student – learned Lorca
from the library stacks,

not lying
on the shag rug
in the lecturer's flat.

I half-listened to his *Verde,*
que te quiero verde,
knowing he would kiss me later;

half-believing that his tongue –
its twist and roll
around my own –

would transmit linguistics,
short-cut me
to fluency.

EXCHANGE

I made him potluck curries,
masala-spicy with a twist of lime
when it seemed he was not going home.

He made me a walnut mantel,
a place for glass to show its colours
over the wood-burning stove.

I made him laugh,
flattered the flick of his chisel,
the burn of his saw.

He made his mark –
his mark was everywhere – this part,
believe me, I did not make up.

He fashioned a partition,
two rooms from one;
he made his side, I made mine.

ROLL UP

Coiled up inside
his new wife

with her high-wire hips
and greasepaint

is a girl – or boy – baby
with hands like his,

hands that could be turned
to anything,

jelly hands turned
to mama still, holding on

for the trapeze act
of a lifetime.

I do not envy her
the canvas stretched

over the Big Top
of her being,

nor the impatient bucking
of its key performer. Once,

I would have entertained
an acrobat or lion tamer,

worn my lips red
and my neckline low

to be somebody
in that ringmaster's show.

MATERNITY

I want to have poems
by Caesarean section
wearing my Infallible lip gloss

and counting on my designer
obstetrician.
I will keep my bump discreet,

drink litres of San Pellegrino,
strive to avoid *striae gravidarum*,
laser them later if it comes to it.

I want to live a normal life
despite the media,
and when it's time,

my lines will glide out raring
to open their lungs and wail
as true as any natural birth.

Japanese Garden

If I'd been a garden
I'd have put down
in Japan,
relished the tickle
of a rake at sunrise,
explained myself
in circles formed in stone.

I'd have been bamboo
and lanterns,
gravel made to look
like water,
full-moon maples
extending
their baby's hands.

WHY

A thoughtful guy, Why,
the kind who can't sit easy
for quizzes and queries puzzling his brow.

How was his childhood sweetheart.
They made out behind the question marks at school.
All the kids knew How and Why.

He begged, *why not forever?*
She said, *that's not how it works.*
She left him soon after for an Easy Answer.

Why me? cried Why.
He'd had some Easy Answers himself,
but they didn't satisfy.

He texted one of the Wherefores of Knocklyon,
they had a pint, made up their minds
that there were more questions than answers.

Building Castles

When I cut the grass
and twigs catch in the blades
the engine stops.

I know I should unplug
before I turn the body on its side,
before I take a risk.

I think of you:
our school excursion
to Bunmahon,

a dull day on the strand,
and you, one of the big girls,
say, let's make a sandcastle.

We kneel to face each other,
you unclip the leather band
of your prosthesis,

lay it down beside you,
its fingers curled,
a Bonsai hand fork;

you nudge and sweep the sand
with thumb and heel of hand,
while the other does the shaping.

I join in, unsure
of my two ordinary hands,
and listen to the story

of the lawnmower.
Does my mouth fall open
as you tell it

or am I old enough
to make believe
such stories sieve

through my ten fingers
every day,
are patted into place?

To Olga

You were the only girl on my wall
a *Jackie* centrefold, a forward split
across the torn-out staples.

At seventeen you back-flipped on the high bar,
back-tucked on the beam, you flew the floor
to bend like Slinky.

Circus-brave, you turned the world's head,
filled each girl's head
with Olympic gold.

I practised handstands, chalked my palms,
I scaled the rope to write your name
on the ceiling.

When you got a nine point eight
in the uneven bars, we all booed
the black-and-white Munich judges –

Give her Ten! In Montreal it was all
about Nadia, girls
and the world are fickle.

Nowadays you live in Arizona
drive a Subaru, teach kids
the Korbut Flip.

Someone called Alyssa posts
that you stole figs, tea, cheese and syrup.
A guy called Christian tells her she's unkind,

even Nixon told you, back when Belarussians didn't cry –
I have always been impressed with your ability
to land on your feet.

Shipwrecked

A Shipwreck Bag was a sack of supplies every Sunday –
bullseyes, fake cigarettes and spicy liquorice pipes,
pink or red beads on the bowl, like my dad's pipe,
which was filled and lit, smoked and re-lit,
smoked and emptied twenty times a day
to the sound of a rattling cough, copious spitting.

His thumb would be black,
his jacket pocket sometimes went on fire,
the Full Bent Cherry-Polished Pipe
left smoking away on its own.
He tapped and pulled and chewed on his pipe
and we tapped and pulled and chewed on ours.

In his sixties he gave it up, buried the pipe
under a rose bush at the Blackrock Clinic,
then closed his eyes as they bypassed his heart.
He developed a sweet tooth like ours,
tasted a handful of years with his mended heart.
But the cough rattled back, too late for a Shipwreck Bag.

GIFTS

The first time we were apart,
you rang from Dallas
full of news about the conference –
lunch with the lads at Hooters
served by busty waitresses.
Three artificial sunflowers
you brought back.

When your mum was fading,
we'd take turns
to brush plump petals
down her face,
to smooth her cheeks
with sunflowers,
yellow, purple, red.

Now the flowers bloom
beside our bed
with a soft dog you brought home
from a Scottish trip.
The real dog and I
permit you to tell stories,
fill our heads with Texan sunshine.

ON INTRODUCING MY HUSBAND TO MY EX

I did not need to say to you,
darling, this is X,
the one who pumped my heart

with helium and cast it,
airborne to the whin,
where it lay punctured,

inhaling yellow,
no longer certain
what it was for;

and this, my love, is Y,
the one who landed my X
while I was still talking funny,

boosted and high.
So much time has passed
that we all feel safe

to come out again,
our adjusted hearts
vacuum-packed against

accidental damage,
but valiant,
curious and light.

THE BEST THING ABOUT HOOVERING

The neat new
  Philips Hoover
    hums me up
      the narrow stairs,
        sucks up all thoughts
          but one:
            the best thing
            about hoovering
            is that spring-loaded
            moment when,
          with deft bare toe to switch,
          the whole long tail of it
        retracts to spindle like a pack
      of greyhounds in rewind,
    that course and nudge
      to form a single beast
        careering backwards
          to the start of time.

        The worst thing
          about hoovering
            is fast-falling
          from the landing
              tangled in the hose,
            wrong-footed by the trim,
        head in the wrong place
          below my feet;
            hands lunging
              for the hundred-year-old spindles
                that can slip
                  or crack
                    or save;
                  my scream,
                he tells me later,
                  is primeval,

prised from
the cave-woman
in my chest.

The best thing about falling
down the stairs
are the sounds
the dog and he make
as I bare my wounds:
a Passion of contralto
and bass-baritone,
a duet worthy
of the Lamentations
of the Prophet Jeremiah.

DOG WHISPERER

He has taken to quoting
from Cesar Millan,
dog whisperer to the stars,
or at least to the dogs
of the stars.

It's all about nose,
then eyes, then ears,
as he sifts the dog's dinner
through his fingers,
folding it with his scent.

He practises the soft bite
on my shoulder,
forming a jaw with his hand,
restrains me as a bitch would her pups;
then practises on the hound.

He turns down the volume
on our favourite series
to nuzzle me gently,
stroke my back, remind me
to get inside the canine mind.

He tries out some whispering
during the ads,
some rehabilitation,
and Minnie does active submission
like she's read the book herself.

Be more like your dog,
he whispers: *forgive, take naps,*
fill your head with every new scent.
She is our Sirius, our summer,
our companion star.

EASTER SUNDAY IN IKEA AND A&E

I was surprised how many people
choose IKEA for their Easter Sunday lunch.
That's where we are when they ring
to say your mum's been taken in.

Abandoning the Easter Sunday marzipan
and meatballs, we buy a Rutger swivel chair,
boxed up so neat we won't know till we're home
its legs are missing. In A&E

the Transfer Letter's been mislaid.
The pregnant doctor barks unanswerable questions
like *can you lift your legs*? Decides to do a reflex test,
applies a pointer to the patient's sole,

she kicks, squeals – *take the gun away*!
The doctor tries the other foot – *the gun! The gun!*
Well, says the doctor, *she can move her legs.*
Nothing can be done until the letter's found.

We pass the trolley hours with the IKEA catalogue,
admire a Manstad corner sofa bed with storage,
praise the finish on the Torsby dining tables.
Clutching a balled-up corner of her sheet

your mother polishes the pages. When we have read
and she has dusted every one, you start to sing.
At *Christ the Lord is Risen Today*
your mother moves her lips.

The lyrics are forgotten, so we hum *A Green Hill
Far Away*, repeatedly, until she sleeps.

RED HEN

We know nothing
about hens, yet find ourselves
in charge of half a dozen.

The odd girl out –
you call her Mrs One – loses
her footing in the mud.

You carry her
into the hen-house
with piano player hands.

Still there the next day,
she has turned her blunt
red beak to the wall.

We talk to neighbours
about red mites, infections,
wonder if she's egg-bound.

We fill her bowl
with cabbage-leaves,
stroke her tight wings.

Her sisters cry out,
foul her water,
shit on her plumage.

We are told you'd get
a new hen for the price
of the vet. For the first time

I want to crack a bird's neck.
Instead we hand her back,
ailing but alive.

Weeks later you find me
in quick tears
for the red hen;

you brush the rust
of my feathers, fill up
my hopper with oyster shells.

END OF THE ROAD

At the Applegreen in Enfield
there's a hearse pulled up.
Did the driver go in for a meal,

or a Crunchie, or did he stop
to GPS, to make enquiries?
Is he unfamiliar with Kilcock?

If so, has he been driving
round the country with a corpse,
feeling lost, which reminds me

of the life-sized torso
laid out bare in the boot
of my old Ford Focus,

its viscera dangling from hooks;
reminds me, too, that Murt's
dad was an undertaker,

how the men from other firms
would park and chit chat
in their limos outside church

but that was not the way of his dad
who would always go in,
who liked to stay close to his dead.

Sign at Crash Repair Garage, Penryn: 'Catalysts Tested'

Elbow to elbow on the Truro train,
I get engaged in conversation,

the kind of chat that happens
when you're squatting on a suitcase.

Hot smells of oil and diesel
remind me of the tantalizing offer

at a garage in Penryn:
'Catalysts tested'.

Can they determine your turning points,
instruct you in advance how

this chance meeting on the Truro train
could convert me so completely

that I'd look back years from now,
confirm – yes, that was the catalyst?

Or if the test of my encounter
read Catalytic Negative, would I

just scribble this guy's number
on the back of my hand, erase it later

with a twist of powdered soap
and burn away the chance?

INTUITIVES

You won't want to know
about the ghost
in your back bedroom,

or that someone jumped
from your first floor flat
onto thirteen granite steps.

Nor is it helpful, after the fact,
to learn the meanings
of numbers:

the icons for endings,
when together,
your lover and you

have succumbed to
a bungalow,
the finality of 9.

It serves no purpose
to know what's coming next:
yet after your lover has left

you'll take a lodger
who every single night
unwraps the Tarot;

you'll draw comfort
from its pentacles,
safety from its swords.

FOOL'S CREDO

I could say that I believe
in the way a song dives behind my ribcage,
and stays there, pounding out its message
for the rest of my body to explain.

I could tell you I believe in the ten point plan,
or that I trust the hymnal, the tarot, the zafu
(on alternating days).

I could say I believe in the truth,
but you'd see through me, see that I'm no more
than an air picked up on the radio,
a transparent kneeling body,

yet the card I've picked reveals a zero,
shows a beggar ready on a precipice,
its message: *hold your nose and jump.*

WINNIE-THE-POOH

To make things all right
he pulls the heavy hardback
from a dusty place.

Once upon a time,
a very long time ago,
about last Friday ...

In the voice reserved
for honey-hungry children
like Christopher Robin and me,

he reads of a craving
for sweetness, of blue balloons
deceiving the bees.

I like that the story
is told just for me, for the you
that is Christopher Robin

or anyone who listens;
told even for
this heffalumpen version

of a girl who heard it first
in the voice her mummy kept
for her kindergarten children,

for the fours and fives and sixes
who believed.

FORMAL APPLICATION
To be undivided must mean not knowing you are
– Jane Hirshfield

Now I am of age
I'd like to get in touch
with my Better Self.
Is she on file at the Department
of Alternative Selves?
Is there a form I can fill in?

Were we divided at birth
or did we rub together
in the same crib, bear
the same christening charms
before each was carried off
on separated ways?

Things being equal,
I want more than reunion;
my true goal
is to hand myself back,
step into her
immaculate groove,

her without-trying-
just-rightness.
I'll live in her,
moment after lucid moment
knowing who I was,
knowing that I am.

AUTOBIOGRAPHY
after Frank O'Hara

When I was a child,
I went by 'Jimmy';
fell from a high wall,
the arrow still in me.

My brother's underpants
with their boastful Y,
fresh from the hot press
I wore them all day.

To be a boy, to be a boy
was all I wanted;
girls set tables,
women waited.

And here I am:
moonstone, mascara;
despite myself, a woman,
mimicking O'Hara!

IT HOLDS NO WATER

It is neither cup
nor jug nor demijohn
neither barrel nor bucket
nor basin nor butt
nor pitcher and ewer
nor firkin nor sump
nor bladder nor kettle
nor goblet nor flask
nor Waterford Glass
nor any other vessel
true to its task.

Your words fall through
the circles of your colander
the basket of your lies
the turlough of your almost-was
your net, your mesh
your gauze;
leave only the sticky
the stubborn, the scrap
your words fall through
– despite your dodging logic –
the unsealed gaps.

ENDING

There is a pleasure in finishing something,
like a roll of dental floss,
apparently everlasting but finally, not.

A novel – yes – that getting to the final page
that gives you all you were holding out for –
ties up, zooms out, or lets you down.

A bar of soap, a victory of sorts for frugality,
for not giving up as the final sliver
dives out of your hands,

has you bend more than once,
risk smacking your head, makes you follow
its last flat holding of juniper.

You may walk around for days, then,
almost remembering to buy more floss,
more soap, recalling the characters,

asking yourself why they did it,
was it really fair to expect you to buy it,
that fast, cheap ending?

But where is the pleasure in finishing this
once-beautiful thing, which is over, not
because no thread or words or fragrance remains,

but is wrapped up, wound down, folded
and closed because it's old or dusty
and has squandered its shine?

DAD'S CANVASSING CARD

The year he went up for election
his photograph was printed in reverse:
the right side of his face on the left
the left side on the right.

His photograph was printed in reverse,
a mirror image of himself,
the left side on the right –
he looked like someone else.

A mirror image of himself:
his film star parting, that dimple,
he looked like someone else
with his *Houses! More Houses! Your Houses!*

His film star parting, that dimple,
you'd vote for those perfect blue eyes.
With his *Houses! More Houses! Your Houses!*
I don't know why he didn't win.

You'd vote for those perfect blue eyes,
but the right side of his face on the left?
I don't know why he didn't win
the year he went up for election.

BEST OF THREE

When it first came in, they'd use cigar box lids
for bats, a champagne cork for a ball.
They played it after dinner, as a parlour game,
the fathers back from India keeping score,
the uncles in their uniforms shaking hands.

Our dad taught us how to hold the blade,
coached us on how the sleight of hand required
to spin the ball depended on your stance,
your handshake grip, the flick of wood and rubber,
showed the three of us the chop, the loop, the kill.

Jack Frost was outside but we were holed up
round the table in the echoing house, and sweating.
Everyone played, even Uncle Arthur, whose hands
big as mill wheels dizzied and spun the spectators,
each grateful for the pipe smoke lightness of the ball.

Last night in the Parochial Lodge, my hands shook
as the ball danced away from me. New rules,
faster, up to eleven only and two serves each.
Slowly I corrected my footing as though
my father still stood by the net, score-keeping.

COME QUIETLY

And then
there are the poems
you shouldn't write,
poems out of uniform
flex crowbars
and flashlights;

secrets that will not
come quietly
are shackled
and coerced –
wary of the promises
that nobody gets hurt.

WALKING OUR DOG TO THE ITALIAN COFFEE SHOP

Her tail spins
at the speed of a Ferrari,

her ears are cones
of equilateral enquiry.

I take my coffee to a sunny bench
to write my diary

she lies beneath
and falls in love entirely

with the bare legs of men
from Cagliari.

LIFE MASK

If I'd been an Amsterdam merchant
I'd have had your features moulded;
mortared to the wall above
our third floor window on the Herengracht
so your nostrils of ceramic might inhale,
as long as these great buildings stood,
black pepper, cinnamon and cassia.

In years to come canal boat tourists,
lit up by The Yellow Sunflowers, thirsty
for the trickle from The Milkmaid's jug,
would marvel at your captain's nose,
those tulip lips, your perfect ears intact.
He never ate bread pudding,
they'd conjecture, *but he never lacked.*

EXECUTOR SALE

The ad said:
approx half an acre,
extensive, magnificent.

A gulp of magpies,
we peck our way
around an empty nest.

The agent has a crooked spine,
eyes of a sparrow hawk,
he flits from our path.

Inside, dark tongues
of floral wallpaper disclose
a smell of mould and must.

A square blue bottle
on the dining table:
Royal Salute Scotch Whiskey, 1801.

A panic button
in the master bedroom;
a cantilevered wheeling table;

depressions in the sand-pink carpet
where the bed's feet stood;
one mustard armchair.

They'll be sold,
jokes a magpie man,
as props for a film.

Here on the sideboard,
a funeral service sheet, inscribed:
With Christ which is far better.

The ad said:
approx half an acre,
extensive, magnificent.

WITH A VIEW TO SETTLING DOWN

Even though I've met you
three, four times,
we have never been alone together.

We touched, of course,
when the agent was engaged
on his phone,

I admired your solid back,
turned on your taps,
held your cold handles.

My warm heart
was rejected out of hand.
Months later, short of suitors,

you began to see me differently,
indulged me ... a rattan chair
in the gold-papered bedroom

where I could fall asleep,
my gaze on the grey-blue hammock
of the Irish Sea.

Today you are mine.
I drive all afternoon
to get to you,

misgivings
like ramps in the road,
prayers that we'll fall in love.

PRESBYTERY CURTAINS

Like the threadbare carpet,
clapped-out cooker, we

are to be thrown in
with the house.

Far from this
our mitred corners.

Did we not pull our weight
for piety, security and insulation?

Far from this
our goblet pleats, our interlining.

All these years
we kept you artful and discreet.

Not once
did we swagger or rail,

not once reveal
the catch behind our nets.

Far from this
our custom finish.

Not for us
to draw conclusions.

FEEDBACK

The reader who texted to say
she'd read the whole book at one sitting.

The reader who admitted
she only likes the sexy ones.

The man who simply said,
the thing is, my dad died too.

The reader who had lost a breast,
and was surprised to hear it spoken of.

The listener who confessed:
your work does nothing for me

on the page;
the listener who left.

The editor who emailed:
please send more.

The old friend who confides
at every public reading,

over the glass
of Lidl Chardonnay

God, I'm glad I never asked you out –
I'd hate to be in any of those poems.

MUSES

Some time after I dropped off,
swaddled in an Autumn duvet,
a Foxford rug already fallen
on the leaf-strewn floor,

the skylight I'd left open
creaked in the breeze,
allowed in poem-flies,
mottled and fizzing

each carrying a word
on its poem-fly back.
They flitted and buzzed
until the room

was swarming
with their arrow selves,
implying, suggesting,
metaphorising, punching,

alliterating, dropping
flecks of pathos and bathos
on the blind as they left.
Late that afternoon,

dry and headachy,
I felt the room had changed –
the laptop I'd shut down
was awake again,

its insect hum
zinging the air.

'A Marriage' is inspired by Anne Stevenson's poem, 'A Marriage', which treats of the poet's parents' relationship and their response to the news that her mother's cancer treatment 'wasn't working', this poem echoes Stevenson's phrase, 'Later, on the porch, alive in the dark together', in its 'Later, intact in the dark together'. Anne Stevenson, *Poems 1955–2005*, Bloodaxe.

'Autobiography' is inspired by Frank O'Hara's (1926–1966) poem, 'Autobiographia Literaria', which begins, 'When I was a child'.

ACKNOWLEDGEMENTS

Grateful acknowledgement is made to the following publications for poems that appeared in them, sometimes in a different form: *Clifden 35, Clockhouse, Five, In Touch* magazine, *Interpreter's House, Kind of a Hurricane, Listowel Writers' Week Anthology 2014, Orbis, Salzburg Review, Signal Arts Magazine, Stand Magazine, The Muse, These Things Happen: Writings from Bray Active Retirement Association*. A version of 'The Dog Whisperer' was chosen for outdoor display by North West Words Poetry for Spaces, Donegal. A version of 'Executor Sale' won first prize in Listowel Writers' Week Originals Single Poem competition, 2014.

Thanks to Rowan Gillespie for his beautiful front cover image, and to Wexford County Council who commissioned 'Solstice'. Thanks also to Caroline Schofield for the haunting back cover drawing.

I wish to thank the following people for their advice and encouragement: my esteemed readers Jane Clarke, Geraldine Mitchell and Katie Donovan; my workshop group Richard Cox, Eithne Hand, Jessica Traynor and Liam Thompson. For her trust in the world of the imagination, and in me as an artist, Eina McHugh. For his steadfast support, valued opinion and so much more, Philip Beck. For taking a chance on my book, Alan Hayes of Arlen House.

Further thanks to the Heinrich Böll committee, Achill, the staff at the Tyrone Guthrie Centre at Annaghmakerrig, Roger McClure, Zandra Carrington, the Arvon Foundation, and the organisers of Key West Literary Seminar, all of whom provided beautiful, supportive spaces in which to write.

Shirley McClure lives in Bray, County Wicklow. Her CD, *Spanish Affair*, with her own poems, plus poetry and music from invited guests, was launched in June 2015, with all proceeds going to Arklow Cancer Support Group, where she facilitates a writers' group. Her first poetry collection, *Who's Counting?* was published by Bradshaw Books and won the *Cork Literary Review*'s Manuscript Competition 2009. She won Listowel Writers' Week Originals Poetry Competition 2014.

www.thepoetryvein.com